The 1890s are an especially interesting time in the history of banking in the United States. The banking system was developing rapidly along with the rest of the economy. It was a turbulent time for the banking system; there were severe strains in the financial sector in 1890 and 1896 and one of the most severe banking panics in US history occurred in 1893 (Calomiris and Gorton 1991; Carlson 2005). This period also affords the opportunity of observing bank risk management and portfolio management practices in an environment of relatively light prudential regulation and no government safety net protection of banks (neither state-level nor federal deposit insurance were available at this time, and the Federal Reserve System had not been founded yet).

The purpose of this paper is to introduce the information contained in an underutilized resource for looking at the banks of this period: the reports filed by the National Bank examiners. These reports contain a significant amount of qualitative and quantitative information not available elsewhere. We describe what the reports reveal about the corporate governance, asset composition, and liabilities structure of National banks. The level of detail provided in the reports makes possible a rich understanding of the condition of the banking system at this time, as well as a wealth of information about the process of banking supervision. Our primary purpose is to characterize the information in the reports and describe the state of the banking system at the time, rather than to formally test any particular hypotheses.

We focus on a sample of 206 banks located in 37 cities during the early 1890s. We chose this particular time period because of the interesting events in the banking system that were occurring, and also because the examination reports became much more detailed around this time. The sample is not random or representative of all National Banks in the United States. It consists of all the National Banks in 37 significant cities located in the middle, South, and West of the country, including many so-called "reserve cities," as defined under the laws governing National Banks. For the sake of comparability, we exclude the very largest cities in these regions (Chicago, St. Louis, and San Francisco) because of the special attributes of banks in those cities (their large size and importance in the interbank deposit market), and the large numbers of banks located in each (the coding of each observation in our sample requires significant effort, and we sought to include a complete list of National Banks in each subject city). The banks in our sample tend to be involved in interbank markets and payment systems at the regional level. Thus we argue the banks in the sample are all in roughly the same peer group; they are of roughly the same size and most seem to be engaged in the interbank market as both holders of deposits of smaller banks and providers of deposits to banks in the central reserve cities. Thus, our sample affords a detailed study of the mid-tier of the National Banks operating during the early 1890s.

Examinations typically took about two days, but could take a bit longer for banks farther west, larger banks, or banks in reserve cities. Banks were typically examined every nine or ten months. Whether all the banks in the town were examined about the same time depended on the number of banks. In towns with fewer banks, they were all examined in short order. If there were many banks, the examiners would look at several of them, leave for a month or so, then return to examine the rest. This approach likely reflected a balancing of the benefits of surprise examination and economizing on time and transport costs.

The material in the examination report covered both the operations of the bank and its balance sheet. It provides information on the ownership, the corporate governance, and management of the bank. Many, but not all, banks were owned substantially by insiders, with the largest shareholder often being the President, although sometimes a board member who was not part of the management team was the largest shareholder. Corporate boards of directors employed several means of regulating and monitoring the behavior of officers including instituting an independent discount committee to examine loans, appointing more independent directors to the board, or requiring various bank officers to post surety bonds. Such practices tended to be more prevalent in the more Eastern and Southern locations within our sample. These findings suggest an evolution in the purpose and obligations of the boards of directors of banks relative to their purpose in the ante-bellum period in the East (Bodenhorn 2013, Hilt 2008, and Lamoreaux 1994).

There is considerable detail about the loan book in the examiner reports. Most loans were made "on time" rather than "on demand" and, while generally not secured by collateral, loans often had a second signatory to ensure payment of the loan. We find that some banks, particularly those farther west, had a considerable portion of their loans in real estate mortgages despite legal prohibitions on originating such loans. Such prohibitions appear to have been evaded by incorporating real estate as secondary collateral after the origination of the loan.

The information about liabilities includes the amounts of each type of liability as well as information about the rates of interest paid. Consistent with other studies of regional differences in interest rates (Davis 1965, Sylla 1969, Smiley 1975, and James 1976), rates paid on time deposits for the banks in our sample tended to be higher farther west. We also learn from the examiner reports about the use of collateralized certificate of deposit as a form of interbank borrowing. This form of borrowing, which examiners viewed as similar to bills payable or rediscounts, had not been noted much previously. We observe that the use of all types of interbank borrowing increased in October and diminished in February, a phenomenon that represents another facet of the seasonality in interest rates and flows of money to and from New

York City during this period that has been noted by others (Kemmerer 1911, James 1978, and Miron 1986).

The examination reports also provide information about the quality of managers, about dividend payments and about examiners' opinions regarding likely losses on different assets. Banks generally paid dividends twice a year. Banks farther west were somewhat more likely to have not paid dividends recently—either because they were new or because they had higher expected losses—but tended to pay higher dividends per share when dividends were paid. Expected losses primarily reflected probable loan losses rather than writedowns of any other type of asset.

The paper is organized to follow the structure of the examination report and proceeds as follows. A more detailed description of the sample is contained in Section 1. Section 2 provides information about the nature of the examinations, such as their length of time and the frequency with which they were conducted. Section 3 describes examination report information relating to ownership and corporate governance. Information about balance sheets is described in Section 4. The examination reports also contained a recapitulation section, which is described in Section 5. Section 6 concludes.

Section 1. Description of our sample

Here we provide a more detailed description of the data sample, both the banks that are included and the time period covered.

The banks in our sample are located in 37 cities in 21 states. The cities are generally larger cities, and include many of the reserve cities, although we also include a few cities of more modest size. A list of the cities we use and their population from the 1890 census is shown in Table 1. The largest city is Cincinnati, OH, which is also one of the most eastern cities; the smallest city is Albuquerque, NM.

We divide the territory of our coverage into four regions: the Ohio River Valley/South (consisting of OH, IN, KY, TN, LA, and AL), the Plains (consisting of IA, MN, MO, NE, and ND), the Mountains/Southwest (consisting of CO, MT, NM, TX, UT, and WY), and the Pacific (consisting of CA, OR, and WA).[1] We investigate how banking practices and behaviors differed across these regions.

Our sample of 206 banks consists of all the National Banks in each of our 37 cities that existed in late 1892 and that had an examination report filed prior to May 1, 1893 (which we take as the start of the Panic of 1893).[2] The distribution of these banks across cities is also shown in Table 1. Cincinnati has the most banks at 13, followed by Denver and Kansas City, Missouri at 11. The largest bank in the sample is also located in Cincinnati, although St. Paul, MN has the largest average size of banks. The smallest bank is located in Rochester, MN.

To establish our snapshot of the banking industry we look at the banking examination report most closely preceding May 1, 1893. Typically these examinations were conducted in late 1892 or early 1893. We also determined when the prior exam took place. We look at this pre-panic period for two reasons. First, in 1891, the comptroller expanded the report from three pages to seven pages, so looking at the examination reports during this period provides considerably more information than was available prior to 1891. (Though in both periods, supplemental pages were sometimes included if the examiner felt a particular need to comment

---

[1] We looked at whether our Southern cities differed from cities in the Ohio River Valley, and found they looked fairly similar. This finding may reflect the fact that New Orleans, which had a long history as a banking center, represents a sizable part of the sample.

[2] In particular, we select banks that filed a call report in September 1892; while we do not use the call report much here, we do so extensively in related work. We do exclude one bank from Kansas City which was chartered in mid-1892, has an exam report in September and early November, and liquidates in mid-November. Given the short life span of the bank, it has an unusual balance sheet and exam profile.

at length about some aspect of the bank.) Second, we would like to gain a better understanding of banking practices in normal times to provide a benchmark for understanding how the banking system might be affected during the panics.

Section 2. Timing and Frequency of the Exam Reports

All of our sample cities contain at least two National Banks, and some cities have as many as thirteen. In cities with a relatively small number of National Banks, the examiner would typically examine all the banks in one visit. In towns with a larger number, say around seven, the examiner would often look at some banks, leave for a time, then return to review the rest during a second visit. For example, in Omaha, four banks were examined in November of 1892 and the remaining five banks were examined in March of 1893. Typically when the examinations for National Banks in a particular location were separated, the break would last about a month, but gaps of three or more months were not uncommon. Although the timing of returns to a city probably were not quite "random" dates for starting the exam, the breaks between the examinations of different subsets of banks within a city likely alleviated some of the window dressing in anticipation of an exam (whereby banks would alter their financial condition once the examiner first appeared in town).

The typical examination in our sample lasted one or two days (with two days being slightly more common than one day—see Table 2). Having the exam take more than 4 days was uncommon and occurred for less than 10 percent of the sample.[3] There was some tendency for larger banks to have longer exams; the typical exam length was roughly one day longer for banks

---

[3] In at least one of these cases, the examiner reported being called away in the middle of the exam to assist with matters at another institution. While some examiners appeared to work on weekends, others did not, which might have contributed to lengthening the observed duration of their exams.

with assets at or above the median of the sample than for banks with assets less than the median in the sample.

In the early 1890s, the Comptroller's office switched from requiring annual to requiring bi-annual examinations.[4] For the banks in our sample, the preceding examination had, on average, occurred about 10 months earlier. However, it was not uncommon for the previous exam to have occurred a little more than one year earlier (the upper quartile for the number of days between exams is 373 days). The frequency of examinations appears to have varied regionally. For banks along the Pacific coast, the median time between exams was just over one year, while for banks in the Ohio River Valley/South, the median time between exams was just under nine months.

The examination reports used here include the work of 20 different examiners. Examiners could cover a wide area; for instance, we observe one examiner covering Alabama, Louisiana, and parts of Tennessee.

Section 3. Ownership Structure, Management, and Corporate Governance

One page of the examination report was devoted to the governance and management of the bank. Examiners were asked to list each member of the Board of Directors, the number of shares of stock in the bank each director held, their city of residence, the amounts they owed to the bank (or the debts of others that they had endorsed), and the other occupation they might have. The examiner was then asked to comment on the oversight exercised by Board: the frequency with which they met, the operations of the independent committees to monitor the bank, and whether the Board had been elected in a proper fashion. Examiners were also asked to

---

[4] See Robertson (1968) for a discussion of the history of the National Banking System and the role of the bank examination process in that context. White (1983) discusses the regulatory environment for both National and state-chartered banks and in particular describes how regulations for state banks varied from state to state.

provide information on the officers of the bank: the President, Vice-President, Cashier (in today's parlance, the Chief Operating Officer of the bank), Assistant Cashier, Teller, and Bookkeeper. The information here included their indebtedness, salaries, surety bonds, if any, as well as general comments on their quality including "whether the officers are capable, prudent, and of good reputation or not, and whether in your opinion, their management is efficient and successful, or otherwise."

Section 3.1. Ownership structure

We classify shareholders into three groups. Our first group consists of management of the bank, particularly the president, vice-president(s), and cashier. The second group of shareholders consists of independent directors, defined as members of the board of directors that were not officers of the bank. (The president of the bank was always on the board and it was not uncommon for at least one other officer to be as well.) The third group consists of the other outside shareholders—non-officers, and non-board members.

The distribution of ownership ranged considerably. As shown in Figure 1, in some banks, the majority of shares were owned by the management while at other banks managers owned almost no bank shares. In our sample of banks, the median ownership share by management was 17 percent, but exceeded 37 percent for one-fourth of the banks in the sample.[5] Management ownership tended to be somewhat higher in the Mountain/Southwest and Pacific parts of the country. Ownership by outside directors tended to be a bit more modest with the median proportion being 12 percent. Outsiders held the remainder. The single largest observed shareholder tended to be the president, which was the case at 60 percent of the banks. However,

---

[5] Thus is appears that, in general, ownership was less concentrated than it had been for banks operating in New York early in the 19th century as reported by Hilt (2008).

at about 30 percent of the banks, an outside director was the largest observed shareholder and at about 10 percent of banks, the cashier was the largest shareholder.

Section 3.2 The Board of Directors

Boards of directors clearly were regarded as important in exercising oversight of the bank. The number of directors varied greatly. In our sample, banks had an average of 9 directors, although some institutions had as many as 23 or as few as 4 (Table 3).[6] Boards tended to be bigger at larger banks and at banks located more to the East.

The majority of the board usually consisted of independent directors (although every bank was required to have at least one independent director). The average portion of the board that consisted of independent directors was a bit more than two-thirds. Independent directors, in theory, acted as the voices of outside shareholders and served on the Board to protect the interests of outside stockholders.[7] Independent directors also traditionally helped attract business to the bank and could provide independent analysis of the creditworthiness of potential borrowers.[8] The occupations of the independent directors in our sample are consistent with these responsibilities.

The most common occupation for the independent directors, as indicated in Table 4, was that of "Capitalist." Presumably such individuals, especially if they were shareholders themselves, would, at least in part, be willing and able to promote actions that would enhance the value of bank shares. Independent directors, of course, like managers, could face conflicts of

---

[6] The average number is quite similar, though the standard deviation considerably larger, to that found by Bodenhorn (2013) for the number of directors on bank boards in mid-Nineteenth century Massachusetts.

[7] In his handbook providing suggestions to national bank shareholders, Coffin (1891) argues that the directors of the National Bank are intended to be the representatives of the shareholders and that shareholders ought to elect individuals whose "integrity, ability and judgment" will best represent their interests.

[8] For instance, the examiner reported that for one bank, "The directors have been selected from the heavy business men of the place, partly for the prestige their names give the bank and partly to obtain their patronage." From the examination report of the Helena National Bank dated January 4, 1893.

interest. In particular, they might themselves be bank borrowers, and thus could conceivably collude with management to receive favorable terms on loans at the expense of shareholders. Indeed, as we discuss below, we find that when boards are dominated by outside directors, outside directors receive more loans from the bank.

Merchants, particularly wholesale merchants, were also a very common occupational category of members on bank boards. Such individuals were also potential customers of the bank and would likely have been particularly aware of shifting business conditions. Thus, they could have fulfilled the goals of attracting business and of advising management about business conditions and the relative merits of different credits.

Lawyers and attorneys were somewhat common as board members, constituting about 7 percent of independent directors. There were some recognizable regional patterns to the occupation of board members, with lumbermen being more common in Minnesota and distillers were listed only in and around Kentucky. One bank in Los Angeles listed both the Governor of the state and a minister among the members of its board. A few notable individuals appear on the boards occasionally; for instance, Messrs. Proctor and Gamble, president and vice-president of a corporation of the same name, appear on the board of the Citizens National Bank of Cincinnati, OH.[9]

By chance, we observe a few instances where officers/directors appear at multiple banks. For instance, the president of the Manufacturer's National Bank in Racine, WI is also president of the First National Bank in Fargo, ND. The president of the First National Bank of Albuquerque, NM is also president of the First National Bank of El Paso, TX. In these cases, it is the cashier who runs the second bank with the President stopping by only a few times a year.

---

[9] Another notable name, Henry Weinhard, brewer, appears on the Board of the Commercial National Bank of Portland, OR. No doubt Mr. Weinhard was an expert on the importance of liquid assets.

We also observe that the President of the Lumberman's National Bank of Stillwater, MN also sits on the Board of the Second National Bank of St. Paul, MN. The examiner's report for Rochester National indicates that the largest stockholder is the estate of the former president (deceased) who apparently owned a few other banks, as well.

Frequently at least some directors borrowed from the bank. On average, about 5 percent of the loans of the bank were to members of the board, although this share reached as high as 27 percent. On average, banks with a higher than median number of directors, a larger than median proportion of independent directors, or a larger than median ownership share by independent directors tended also to show a higher proportion of loans to independent directors (Table 5). Interestingly, there was little regional variation in such lending.[10]

Most commonly, board meetings were held monthly, but weekly or quarterly meetings were also common (Table 6). At a considerable number of banks, the meeting frequency was reported as "Irregular," much to the disapproval of the examiner. Frequent meetings were more common in the Ohio River Valley/South region where nearly one-third of the banks had weekly board meetings. Meetings were less frequent farther west, with quarterly meetings being the second most common frequency in the Plains and Mountain/Southwest regions. While nearly half of the banks in the Pacific had monthly meetings, the second most common frequency was "Irregular" at 17 percent.

Independent discount committees that reviewed the new loans being extended were an important part of corporate governance. Such committees were present at about 60 percent of

---

[10] Insider lending has received considerable attention in studies of early banking in the United States. For instance, Lamoreaux (1994) argues that ante-bellum banks in New England were in large part loan clubs where a considerable portion of the banks' lending was to the members of the Board of Directors. Lamoreaux argues that such lending declined as a share of lending over the 19th Century and finds that by the 1890s only about 9 percent of loans were to members of the Board, a number similar to what we find here (especially if we include the bank officers that also served on the Board).

the banks. At the remaining institutions, the examiner indicated that the discount committees were inactive and that management was left to the officers. There is clear regional variation in the use of such committees. An overwhelming majority of banks in the Ohio River Valley/South had them, while only a minority of the banks in the Mountain/Southwest did. Reserve city banks were also more likely to have independent committees than other banks.

Examiners were also asked to make notes about the annual meetings. In nearly all cases annual meetings and the election of directors was described as regular. The number of shares being represented, either in person or by proxy, was listed.

Section 3.3 Management

The three primary officers were the President, Vice-President(s), and Cashier. There were a number of instances in which there were multiple assistant cashiers, tellers, or bookkeepers, especially in the larger banks; in small banks some of these latter positions were vacant.

The examination reports provide useful information on compensation. Presidents had the highest average salaries at $4,416. The average salaries for the cashiers at $3,416 slightly exceeded those of the vice presidents at $3,113. Salaries of the Presidents, Vice Presidents, and Cashiers topped out at $50,000, $9,000, and $20,000, respectively. On occasion it was noted that one or more of the top three officers did not received any fixed salary. Not surprisingly, salaries were much higher at larger banks, at reserve city banks, and in more eastern parts of the country.

Requiring officers to post surety bonds was a fairly common practice. These bonds could be seized by the bank shareholders (or bank receiver) in the event that the officer posting the bond committed some offence, such as fraud or absconding with funds. Bonds could be personal (backed by assets held in escrow) or provided through a surety company.[11] Given that the cashiers were typically responsible for overseeing the books, and given that they therefore enjoyed ample opportunity to commit fraud or hide funds, it is not be surprising that the cashiers were the class of officers that posted bonds most frequently (60 percent). The Presidents and Vice-presidents posted bonds somewhat less frequently (35 percent and 15 percent of the time, respectively).[12] The bonds were typically about 5 to 10 times the salary of the individual in question. In addition to checking whether the bonds were posted, the examiners also verified that the bonds were being held by someone other than the individual posting the bond.

Mirroring the phrasing of the question on the examination form that the examiners were asked to address, officers were typically described as "capable, prudent, and of good reputation." It seems that so long as the bank was profitable, the management was described as efficient and successful. In only 13 percent of cases did the examiners indicate that they had concerns about the officers. When concerns arose, examiners would point to inexperience, excessive salaries, having outside interests that took too much of their attention, or a lack of prudent management. (Frequently there were other problems at these banks as well, with troubled loans and expected losses on assets tending to be higher on average.) In one case the examiner flagged the personal reputation of the management in matters other than banking, stating that: "officers appear capable and rather prudent. President and cashier have the reputation of being fond of 'women and wine.' Other officers of good reputation."[13]

---

[11] For more information about surety bonds, especially those provided by surety companies, see Lunt (1922).
[12] It was uncommon for the President or Vice-President to be bonded if the cashier was not, but it did happen in a few instances.
[13] Examiner report of the City National Bank of Dallas, TX dated February 23, 1893.

Section 4. The Balance Sheet

Here we review the information contained in the bank balance sheet that was included in the examination reports.

Section 4.1 Loans

Loans accounted for about 60 percent of assets, on average. Commensurately, a considerable portion of the examination report was devoted to discussing the loan book. Examiners were first asked to provide a numerical overview of the loan book and then to provide more descriptive information.

The numerical information took the form of a table that classified loans based first on their type and then on their quality. Loan type was based on whether the loans were "on demand" and could be called at any time by the bank, "on time" with a fixed maturity date, and whether the loans were secured, either by collateral or by other individuals who might act as guarantors. These exclusive categories were (with each average share in brackets):

A: on demand, paper with one or more individual or firm names [7.2%]
B: on demand, secured by stocks, bonds, and other personal securities [5.3%]
C: on time, paper with two or more individual or firm names [38.5%]
D: on time, single-name paper (one person or firm) without other security [22.8%]
E: on time, secured by stocks bonds and other personal securities [21.1%]
F: on time, on mortgages or other real estate security [3.6%]

For the quality assessments, examiners were asked to determine whether the loans were past due according to statutory criteria and whether loans were overdue for other reasons. These two categories appeared on the table as items:

G: bad debts, as defined in section 5204, Revised Statutes [1.9%]
H: Other suspended or overdue paper [7.1%]

Examiners were also asked to note loans to directors. The numbers here should (and did) match those reported in the discussion of the management and were reported as item:

I: Liabilities of directors (individual and firm) as payers [8.3%]

Items G,H, and I were subsets of items A-F.

As is clear from the numbers above that, most of the loans made during this period were time loans that were not formally secured by collateral. However, these loans often had a second signatory to whom the bank could turn in case the primary borrower was unable to pay. Demand loans, where the bank could demand repayment at any time, were generally not a large part of the loan portfolio but were somewhat more common in the Ohio River Valley/South and the Pacific parts of the country (Table 7).[14] Some contemporaries indicated that these loans may have served as a secondary liquidity reserve because banks could call these loans in as needed (Moulton 1918). However, at some banks, demand loans might be less liquid because they consisted partly of loans that had previously matured but whose borrowers were having difficulty repaying; restructuring the loans into demand loans was a way of allowing the loan to stay current while still allowing the bank to exert discipline on the borrower. Although National Banks were prohibited from originating mortgage loans, mortgages and real estate loans appear to have been a non-negligible part of the banks' loan portfolios; we discuss these further below.[15]

During the National Banking Era, banks were not supposed to make loans to any single counterparty for more than 10 percent of the banks' paid-in capital. This rule apparently was not strictly enforced: a bit more than half of the banks in our sample had at least one "excessive"

---

[14] See also James (1978, especially pages 54-71) for a discussion of different types of loans.
[15] While examiners regularly reported the interest rates paid on several types of liabilities, they only infrequently provided details on the interest rates charged on loans. The few reported rates for time loans were around 10 percent. Interest rates on overdrafts were apparently quite a bit higher with rate of 12 or 24 percent reported. The rates we find on loans are generally consistent with other reports for the time such as James (1978) and White (2001).

loan. Examiners for the most part chided the banks for having excessive loans, but unless they were substantial in number, examiners did not often demand that these "excessive" loan amounts be reduced. Sometimes it was noted that the state-chartered banks with whom the National Banks were competing did not face such loan limits so that the National Banks needed to be able to extend such loans in order to remain competitive.

As part of the more descriptive information included in the report, examiners were asked to comment on the overall quality of the loan portfolio as well as whether it was well distributed. Examiners were generally favorably impressed with loan quality. They characterized the quality of loans as something other than good—such as poor or fair—for just 28 banks (although for 14 banks an overall characterization could not be determined from the examiner's comments). So long as the bank did not have too many excess loans, its loans were described as well distributed.

Troubled loans typically constituted about 10 percent of loans. The loan portfolios of banks in the Mountain/Southwest and Pacific regions tended to have a greater proportion of troubled loans than banks in other regions. Examiners also were asked to provide descriptive comments on suspended or overdue paper; the comments that were provided varied substantially across examiners and we found it difficult to devise a way to usefully capture the information that was provided.[16]

Nearly 70 percent of the banks in the sample had at least some loans secured by mortgages or real estate. Although banks were prohibited from originating such loans, banks were allowed to take real estate as (additional) collateral for loans already extended (Coffin 1896, Paine 1914). Of banks that held mortgages, the average number was 5 such loans, although one bank held 47. The average share of loans that consisted of real estate loans was 3.6

---

[16] Though sometimes these notes produced some colorful comments such as from the examiner report of the First National Bank El Paso, TX dated June 20, 1892 that "suspended debts $1500 due since May 1891, maker in jail for murder forcing collection from surety."

percent, but the proportion reached as high as 50 percent. The proportion of the loan portfolio that consisted of mortgages was lowest in the Ohio River Valley/South (at about 2 percent of loans) at highest in the Pacific (at 7 percent). The distributions of real estate loans by region are shown in Figure 2.

The final part of the loan book that was discussed was the use of overdrafts. Most examiners commented on whether the overdrafts were granted "habitually" to the bank's customers (a practice that was frowned upon) and whether the overdrafts were secured. The practice of allowing habitual overdrafts was much more common in the Mountain/Southwest than in other parts of the country. As with "excessive" loans, examiner commentary suggests that National Banks adopted overdraft lending in large part because it was common at banks with which they were competing, mostly unsecured; one examiner reported that the overdrafts were "Habitually granted according to Western custom and in competition with state banks."[17] Bank officials sometimes worried that they would lose customers if they did not grant overdrafts.

> [Overdrafts] Not secured, habitually granted, all temporary but allowed by the president [out of] fear of losing a customer. Some of the parties are chronic in overdrawing and always in red, that being their favorite color. The only recompense the officers have is to collect from the 24% interest while balance is running. Book keeper said not a bad account among them[18]

Overdrafts were generally reported to be unsecured.

Section 4.2 Reserves

Examiners were asked to provide information on bank's reserves and how recent levels—both its current level and average over the past 30 days—compared with the required reserve holdings. (The reserve ratio was defined as cash and balances at reserve banks relative to

---

[17] From the examiner report of the Commercial National Bank of Salt Lake City, UT, dated August 3, 1892.
[18] From the examiner report of the Albuquerque National Bank of Albuquerque, NM, dated July 4, 1892.

individual deposits plus net interbank deposits, with some adjustments allowed for National Bank notes and items due from clearinghouses. For banks located in reserve cities, the reserve requirement was 25 percent and for other banks the reserve requirement was 15 percent.) The reserve ratio exceeded the legal requirement most of the time but was deficient at the time of the exam for about 18 percent of the banks in our sample. Figure 3 shows a histogram of the amount by which the average 30 day reserve ratio reported by the examiners exceeded the legal requirement (the 30 day average ratio was provided for 156 of our 207 banks); we focus on the excess reserve as banks in different cities were subject to different requirements.[19] For the median bank in our sample where the reserve ratio was reported, the reserve held by the bank exceeded the legal requirement by 6.25 percentage points. For about 10 percent of banks the reserve ratio exceeded the required ratio by at least 25 percentage points. Clearly, for many banks, their holdings of reserves were dictated by business considerations (for example, for controlling risk or signaling the quality of their risk management to their depositors) rather than by regulatory requirements. In general, banks in reserve cities tended to hold smaller buffers than banks in country towns.

Section 4.3 Other assets

Examiners listed the stocks, securities, and other claims held by the banks. Claims could include judgments against other parties arising from court decisions. Examiners were asked to list the book value and the current market value. Generally items were held at roughly their market value, although for about 17 percent of banks in the sample, the examiner noted that the

---

[19] Actually, the 30 day ratio is not reported for that many banks. In a few cases the examiner reported instead the ratio for that day and stated it was pretty close to the average. When the 30 day average is missing but a examination day number is reported, we use the one day number.

bank held too many securities that were booked at values in excess of market values or were of questionable value.

Examiners were also asked to provide information on deposits due from reserve agents, banks, and bankers as well as to comment on cash items. With respect to due from other banks, examiners often simply noted that they were seeking verification on items due from other institutions; comments, where provided, might note the number of banks that owed funds to the bank being examined. Occasionally, copies of the form letters sent to correspondents to verify funds were included with the report. Cash items included checks due on local banks, any disputed items (sometimes forged items), and occasionally expense items; the latter two items were required to be written off by the bank. Often the examiner would simply describe cash items as "regular."

The condition of the banking house was also covered in the exam. Most banking houses were described as "suitable and convenient" with a vault and safe that were "good and secure." In a few cases, the examiner indicated that the bank had an overly expensive banking house (possibly a management perquisite taken at the expense of shareholders). In one case the examiner expressed the concern that "While vault and safe are secure, I am compelled to say their banking room is in bad shape as it has been allowed to go so long without repair that the walls are dirty and dingy and in many places the plastering has fallen off and it needs fixing up badly.[20]" Examiners also indicated whether the furniture and fixtures were worth book value or whether their values needed to be written down.

In a few cases, an examiner would note that the bank shared offices with another financial institution, typically a state-charted savings bank, which would have overlapping management. The examiners often expressed concerns about this arrangement. In a few

---

[20] Examiner report of the National Bank of Commerce of Omaha, NE dated March 21, 1893

exceptional cases, it appears that there was incomplete separation of the two financial institutions.

> The business of the People's Savings Bank of Denver, which is under the same management, is conducted in the same room as the banking office and the counter and vaults are used in common. The business of the savings bank appears to be about as active as that of the national bank. If for any cause a run should be made on the savings bank, no doubt the national bank would be affected thereby as the business of the two institutions appear to be as closely connected.[21]

The last asset item that was discussed was the banks' holdings of "Other Real Estate and Mortgages Owned." Typically these were properties acquired when a loan went bad. Among banks that owned such real estate the average number of properties held was 4 and the value of the loans associated with these properties represented, on average, about 3.5 percent of loans. Typically the value of real estate owned exceeded the indebtedness of the borrowers that had pledged the real estate as collateral.

Section 4.4 Capital account and earnings

As part of their discussion of the capital account of the bank, examiners were asked to verify that the ledgers containing the identity of stockholders were correct and that surrendered stock certificates were properly canceled. Under National Bank law at the time stockholders suffered the risk of double-liability: stockholders could be assessed to cover capital impairments or short-falls to liability holders in the event of a receivership in an amount equal to their interest in the bank's paid in capital. As noted by Bolles (1890), the bank ledgers were the source for the identities of the shareholders. The examiners found that the ledgers were generally kept correctly and in only two instances were stock certificates reported as signed in blank (which enabled the stock to be more easily sold but made it more difficult to determine the identity of

---

[21] From the examiner report of the People's National Bank of Denver dated April 18, 1893. As described by Carlson (2005), runs on the savings banks did indeed have negative effects on the associated banks during the crisis of 1893.

the holder). Examiners also reported on whether the bank held its own stock as collateral for loans or otherwise; about 13 percent of banks were reported to do so.

The examination reports also contained information on when the most recent dividend had been paid, whether profits were carried through to surplus, and whether profits were used to charge-off losses or to write down the value of securities or the banking house. Examiners could also note whether they thought that there was a reason that the bank should not pay a dividend during the upcoming period. Nearly 70 percent of banks had paid a dividend within the 6 months prior to the exam (Table 8). Those dividends were, on average, about $5 per share. Dividends were somewhat less likely to have been paid recently in the Mountain/Southwest and Pacific parts of the country, but when they were paid, tended to be a bit higher in terms of dollars per share. About three-fourths of banks had recently used profits to write off at least some losses. Examiners generally did not see much reason for banks to refrain from paying dividends. They provided a reason for not doing so at about 16 percent of the banks in our sample, most commonly noting that the bank was fairly new and needed to build up its surplus, that the banks needed to deal with accumulated bad assets, or that it should restore the surplus after having used it to write down bad assets.

Section 4.5 Liabilities

Much of the remainder of the report concerned the structure of liabilities. Examiners first commented on money that the bank owed to other banks and whether this took the form of "open accounts" (most common) or certificates of deposit (less common). The examiners' reports indicate that most banks that took deposits from other banks and paid interest did so at a rate of 2 percent at this time. James (1978) notes that New York banks also paid a rate of 2 percent on correspondent balances; it is interesting that this rate appears to have been fairly common across the country and did not vary regionally, unlike some other rates. Examiners then reported on deposits more generally. Some detailed information on the constituent parts of individual deposits was included in the examination report. As reported in Table 9, the bulk of deposits were checking accounts (74 percent), followed by demand certificates (14 percent) and time certificates (11 percent). Time and demand certificates of deposit were not much used in the Ohio River Valley/South, but accounted for 25 to 35 percent of individual deposits in other parts of the country.

The examination reports also provide some information on the cost of different types of funds. Interest was almost never paid on checking accounts. Public funds were an important source of funding for banks and these accounts did bear interest. Some public accounts were very large and the examiners would comment if the bank appeared overly dependent on them.

Examiners reviewed the certificates of deposit (CDs), and checked whether the certificate books were properly kept. The rate of interest on CDs was also often recorded. The average rate paid on CDs in late 1892 and early 1893 was about 4 percent, although it reached as high as 7 percent. Some examiners reported that the banks offered CDs of several maturities and that they paid a lower rate for CDs with a shorter maturity (typically around 3 months) and a higher rate for CDs with longer maturities (around 6 months). There was also some regional variation: rates were lowest in the Ohio River Valley/South with particularly low rates being paid by banks in Cincinnati (at 1 percent) and Indianapolis (at 2¾ percent). Rates moved up progressively with distance west with banks on the Pacific, particularly Oregon and Washington, paying the most (in excess 5 percent). The regional patterns are consistent with previous work on interregional interest rate variation (Davis 1965, Sylla 1969, Smiley 1975, and James 1976). That the regions with the highest level of interest rates are also those where troubled loans were a greater share of the portfolio and where dividend payments were more infrequent, is also consistent with the idea in Odell (1989) that some of the differences in interest rates may reflect differences in risk.

Borrowing from other banks received special attention. Such borrowing tended to carry higher interest rates and involved collateral and was generally viewed negatively by examiners. While borrowing in the form of bills discounted or rediscounted has been discussed in other academic work and appears on the call reports, the examiner reports indicate that banks also borrowed from each other via CDs. These CDs were collateralized (unlike CDs issued to individuals), apparently carried higher rates of interest, and were viewed by examiners as similar to other forms of borrowings from banks. Fifteen percent of banks borrowed from other banks using CDs while about one-third of banks were reported to have borrowed money from other banks in any form (bills discounted, rediscounts, or CDs issued for the purpose of borrowing money). Lockhart (1921) claims that there was some stigma associated with borrowing from other banks and that banks would sometimes borrow using CDs because such borrowing was not grouped with other interbank borrowing on the call report and thus enabled banks to disguise the full extent of their interbank borrowing.[22] Consistent with Lockhart's claim, some examiners noted that this form of borrowing was reported with individual deposits by the bank.

As shown in Figure 4, there appears to have been a strong seasonality in the use of interbank borrowing. The fraction of banks using borrowed money is elevated from October to February and is fairly modest for much of the rest of the year (there is a spike in July, although we have somewhat fewer observations in this month). The seasonal needs for rediscounts and

---

[22] Lockhart (1921) also notes that the National Banking act restricted bank indebtedness, other than through notes and deposits, to be no more than paid-in capital which created an additional incentive for banks to not reveal the extent of their interbank indebtedness.

other borrowing was noted by the examiners.[23] For instance in November of 1892 the examiner looked at the First National Bank of Minneapolis and had this to say:

> The business of the bank is very large. I consider its condition good and prosperous although while I think it has too much borrowed money, one can hardly see how it can be avoided. It takes a great deal of money to handle the wheat, lumber, and flour at this point. The regular customers of the bank are largely of this class and they expect their full lines or nearly so of discounts at this season of the year and the management feels as though they must accommodate when possible. Toward Spring the reserve is usually the condition and the money comes back. I suggested to the cashier that perhaps it would be better to carry certificates of deposit that were issued for the purpose of borrowing money as bills payable.[24]

The rates paid on money borrowed from other banks were typically around 6 percent, although they reached as high as 10 percent for some banks while a few banks were able to borrow in this way for as little as 4 percent. Among banks that borrowed, most amounts were fairly modest with the average amount being about 6 percent of assets. However, a few banks were heavy borrowers with borrowings by one bank amounting to almost 20 percent of assets. Examiners reported that such borrowing had been explicitly approved by the board of directors in nearly two-thirds of the cases where examiners commented on this topic. Banks often obtained funds through rediscounts or through borrowing on CDs from banks in New York City, another indication of the importance of institutions in New York in providing liquidity to the banking system at this time. Borrowing was also done, but to a lesser degree, from banks in the other Central and the regional reserve cities (Chicago, St. Louis, San Francisco) and occasionally from other local banks or from country banks located in a distant part of the country.

---

[23] The seasonality is consistent with reports elsewhere such as James (1978),
[24] Examiner report of the First National Bank of Minneapolis, MN dated November 14, 1892.

Section 5. Recapitulation

The final portion of the examination report was a recapitulation. Part of the recapitulation consisted of a table providing the examiner's estimate of losses and necessary write-downs on loans, securities, or other assets. These losses were compared to surplus, and undivided profits, after accounting for other expenses, to determine if the bank's capital was impaired. The recapitulation also included a narrative description of the condition of the bank that included any recommendations about regulatory measures that should be taken in the event the bank was having difficulties. These steps could include the suspension of dividends, or in extreme cases, write-downs of capital and assessments of stockholders.

Most banks were successful, with expenses running lower than undivided profits for all but a handful of banks. Losses for our sample of banks, shown in Table 10, also tended to be small and were less than 15 percent of surplus and undivided profits for three-fourths of the banks. In 13 cases the examiner indicated that the capital of the bank was impaired.

Losses were reported for several categories of assets including "bad loans," other loans, securities, banking house, furniture and fixtures, and other real estate and mortgages. Most losses were related to loans, although examiners did recommend writing down the value of the banking house or "fixtures and furniture" in several cases. As examiners reported both the book value of the various asset categories, it is possible to gauge the loss rates that were expected. The median loss rate on loans across the banks in our sample (in cases where losses were expected to occur) was about 10 percent of the book value of the loans.

Examiners could note in the recapitulation whether banks faced sufficient troubles that they should be disciplined in some way. If there were only a few troubled assets, the examiner would often recommend that those specific assets be charged off; bank officials were generally willing to comply with these recommendations. In cases where problems were more substantial, one of the most typical sanctions was to recommend the suspension of dividend payments. As noted above in Section 4.4, examiners recommended this for a modest portion of the banks in our sample. In some cases, the bank officers indicated that they would voluntarily suspend dividend payments to either charge off bad assets or rebuild their surplus; in these cases, the examiner would often not comment on whether he would also recommend the stopping of dividend payments. The examiner sometimes expressed the opinion that the management ought to be replaced, but also made clear that it was the responsibility of the Board of Directors to determine whether any change would be made.

There were 13 banks for which the examiner considered problem assets to be so substantial that the capital of the bank was impaired. In several of these cases, the examiner noted that the management had recently been replaced and expressed the opinion that the new management would likely help put the bank on better footing. There were three cases, however, where the examiner made exceptional recommendations. One examiner recommended that the bank charge off bad loans against surplus and capital and then permanently reduce capital (by returning some funds to shareholders); reductions in capital would reduce the maximum loan size that the bank could make and presumably result in a smaller bank (as the bank moved toward a more normal leverage ratio with the smaller capital).[25] In a second case the examiner recommended an assessment against capital. In the third case, the examiner recommended the appointment of a receiver.

> The general condition of the bank is bad and its business is not prosperous. It is impossible for me to make an intelligent estimate of the losses that the bank will probably meet on its assets. So much of its funds are tied up in real estate that has no market value now but some of these properties may and probably shall at some time become very valuable. The amounts I have put down as probably losses is

---

[25] See Paine (1914, especially pages 80-82) for discussion of assessments against deficiencies.

surely low enough and it would not astonish me it fully one-half of the capital of the bank is finally lost…Its capital is badly impaired and it would, I think, be better for the reputation of the [National Banking] system if the bank were placed in the hand of a receiver but it would cause great loss to the shareholders and make much trouble here if the receiver tried to realize on the real estate paper. It is shameful and wicked that so much money should be fooled away in so short a time and prove the folly of having real estate speculators as manager of banking institutions.[26]

In the narrative descriptions, banks that were doing well often were characterized favorably in the recapitulation using statements similar to "bank is in a sound and healthy condition and its business is prosperous.[27]" Banks that were not doing as well were characterized less charitably. "This bank's wretched condition appears to have been caused by inefficient management particularly in granting large lines of credit without adequate security…[28]" One simple way of summarizing some of the information in the descriptive section is to note whether the examiner criticized the management, the asset quality, or both. Out of the 205 banks where comments were made (no comments were provided for 1 bank), management problems were cited 19 times and asset quality issues 35 times. As might be expected, problems with management, and especially with asset quality, were more likely when estimated losses were higher.

In addition to the quality of the bank's management and assets, some descriptions contained other useful information. For example, some comments discuss the competitive environment:

General condition of the bank is good but the competition of the old established institutions prevent it from making much money. The banks here are all fighting for business and too many concessions are made to borrowers. Overdrafts are

---

[26] Examiner report of the Washington National Bank of Tacoma, WA dated December 28, 1892.
[27] This one from the examiner report of the United States National Bank of Portland, OR dated April 11, 1893.
[28] Examiner report of the Bankers and Merchants National Bank of Dallas, TX dated November 8, 1892.

seldom refused and paper is allowed to run as long as the borrower wants it without renewal. It is the custom of the place and all the banks follow it.[29]

Other comments provide information about local economic conditions.

Bad paper in the bank is largely a relic of the past - the boom of the city and [subsequent] harder time especially among real estate men from whom the greater part of these losses come. The management is exerting itself in every way by suit and otherwise to force collections and reduce this amount of past due paper. General business is very large and active and its earnings capacity good as will be seen from the statement of profit since July 1, 1892.[30]

[The] bank is gradually coming into good condition and its business is improving. While property is still greatly depreciated there seems to be a marked improvement in affairs in and about San Diego within the last nine or ten months. Business generally has considerably improved, the back country is filling up with settlers, a large amount of land has been planted to citrus and deciduous fruit trees and a large area will come into bearing with the year. The hotels are filled to overflowing with Eastern tourists, many of them investing. Indebtedness is being gradually liquidated and much property is getting into hand of strong holders.[31]

These sorts of comments provide useful characterizations of the banking environment, but are not easily categorized or quantified.

Section 6. Conclusion

The examination reports discussed here provide considerable insight into the banking system of the early 1890s. They help improve our understanding of the examination process and the oversight being exercised by the Office of the Comptroller of the Currency. They also help illuminate the management and governance of the banks, the characteristics of their loan portfolio, and more about the nature of their liabilities.

As highlighted in this article, there tended to be regional differences in the banking environment. The Ohio River Valley/South is characterized by greater scrutiny by examiners,

---

[29] Examiner report of the American National Bank of Helena, MT dated January 6, 1893.
[30] Examiner report of the National German American Bank of St. Paul, MN dated November 28, 1892.
[31] Examiner report for the Consolidated National Bank of San Diego dated February 27, 1893.

more oversight by boards of directors, less ownership by management, less risk taking, and fewer problem assets. Perhaps as a consequence, these banks paid less to borrow funds. Moving west across the country, there appears to be less frequent scrutiny by examiners, more violations of the banking rules, less formal oversight by boards and greater ownership by management, more risk taking, more problem assets, and greater returns to shareholders (when dividends are paid). The commentary from the examination reports suggests that some of the banking practices observed in the western parts of the country reflected competition from nearby banks that were subject to less stringent rules than the National Banks.

References

Bodenhorn, Howard (2013). "Large Block Shareholders, Institutional Investors, Boards of Directors and Bank Value in the Nineteenth Century." *NBER working paper 18955.*

Bolles, Albert (1890). *The National Bank Act and Its Judicial Meaning,* Homans Publishing Company: New York.

Calomiris, Charles W., and Gary Gorton (1991). "The Origins of Banking Panics: Models, Facts, and Bank Regulation," in *Financial Markets and Financial Crises*, R. Glenn Hubbard, ed., University of Chicago Press, 109-73.

Carlson, Mark (2005), "Causes of Bank Suspensions in the Panic of 1893," *Explorations in Economic History,* 42: 56-80.

Coffin, George (1891). *Handbook for National Bank Shareholders, Their Legal Rights and Liabilities Defined,* H.L. McQueen, Washington DC.

Coffin, George (1896). *Handbook for Bank Officers.* McGill and Wallace: Washington DC.

Davis, Lance (1965). "The Investment Market, 1870-1914," *Journal of Economic History,* 24: 355-399.

Hilt, Eric (2008). "When did Ownership Separate from Control? Corporate Governance in the Early Nineteenth Century," *Journal of Economic History,* 68(3): 645-685.

James, John (1976). "The Development of the National Money Market, 1893-1911." *Journal of Economic History,* 36: 878-897.

James, John (1978). *Money and Capital Markets in Postbellum America*, Princeton University Press: Princeton.

Kemmerer, Edwin (1911). *Seasonal Variations in Demands for Currency and Capital.* National Monetary Commission: Washington, DC.

Lamoreaux, Naomi (1994). *Insider Lending,* Cambridge University Press, Cambridge.

Lockhart, Oliver (1921). "The Development of Interbank Borrowing in the National System, 1869-1914," *Journal of Political Economy,* 29(2): 138-160.

Lunt, Edward (1922). *Surety Bonds.* The Ronald Press Company: New York.

Odell, Kerry (1989). "The Integration of Regional and Interregional Capital Markets: Evidence from the Pacific Coast, 1883-1913." *Journal of Economic History,* 49(2): 297-310.

Miron, Jeffrey (1986). "Financial Panics, the Seasonality of the Nominal Interest Rate, and the Founding of the Fed," *American Economic Review*, 76(1): 125-40

Moulton, H. G. (1918). "Commercial Banking and Capital Formation," *Journal of Political Economy,* 26(7): 705-731.

Paine, Willis (1914). *The Laws of the United States Relating to National Banks,* Baker, Voorhis, & Co. New York.

Robertson, Ross (1968). *The Comptroller and Bank Supervision, A Historical Appraisal,* Office of the Comptroller of the Currency: Washington DC.

Smiley, Gene (1975). "Interest Rate Movement in the United States, 1883-1913," *Journal of Economic History,* 35: 591-620.

Sylla, Richard (1969). "Federal Policy, Banking Market Structure, and Capital Mobilization in the United States, 1863-1913," *Journal of Economic History,* 29: 657-686.

White, Eugene (1983). *The Regulation and Reform of the American Banking System, 1900-1929.* Princeton University Press: Princeton.

White, Eugene (2001). "California Banking in the Nineteenth Century: The Art and Method of the Bank of A. Levy," *Business History Review* 75(Summer).

Table 1 – Cities and Banks Used in the Sample

State	City	Population 1890	Number banks	Ave. assets ($k)	Min. assets ($k)	Max. assets ($k)
Alabama	Birmingham	26,178	4	962	342	1,617
Alabama	Mobile	31,076	2	968	369	1,568
California	Los Angeles	50,395	4	1,320	578	2,264
California	San Diego	16,307	2	964	786	1,143
Colorado	Denver	106,713	11	2,768	993	5,695
Colorado	Pueblo	24,558	6	1,016	229	3,055
Indiana	Indianapolis	105,436	5	2,513	1,840	4,076
Iowa	Des Moines	50,093	4	1,145	906	1,282
Iowa	Dubuque	30,311	3	1,138	407	1,558
Kentucky	Lexington	35,698	7	681	295	1,353
Kentucky	Louisville	161,129	10	1,824	1,018	3,726
Louisiana	New Orleans	242,039	10	2,719	962	5,976
Minnesota	Minneapolis	164,738	7	2,725	510	6,100
Minnesota	Rochester	5,321	3	415	164	651
Minnesota	St. Paul	133,156	5	4,581	1,516	6,768
Minnesota	Stillwater	11,260	2	1,285	1,195	1,376
Missouri	Kansas City	132,710	10	3,072	401	7,734
Missouri	St. Joseph	52,324	4	2,242	1,880	2,438
Montana	Helena	13,834	6	1,845	327	4,388
Nebraska	Lincoln	55,164	5	1,050	516	2,525
Nebraska	Omaha	140,452	9	2,633	646	6,669
New Mexico	Albuquerque	3,785	2	878	536	1,220
North Dakota	Fargo	5,664	4	673	389	1,257
Ohio	Cincinnati	290,908	13	4,060	1,312	8,308
Oregon	Portland	46,385	8	1,424	355	4,558
Tennessee	Knoxville	22,535	6	735	244	1,377
Tennessee	Memphis	64,495	4	1,515	1,246	1,727
Tennessee	Nashville	76,168	4	2,765	2,366	3,247
Texas	Dallas	38,067	9	987	288	2,001
Texas	El Paso	15,678	3	554	451	625
Texas	San Antonio	37,673	5	744	232	1,781
Utah	Salt Lake City	44,843	6	1,134	551	2,293
Washington	Spokane	19,922	7	677	423	1,019
Washington	Tacoma	36,006	8	775	269	1,329
Wisconsin	Milwaukee	204,408	3	3,510	2,596	4,716
Wisconsin	Racine	21,014	3	1,102	756	1,468
Wyoming	Cheyenne	11,690	2	849	720	978
	All		206	1,862	164	8,309

Note. Assets here are based on 1892 Call Report to avoid seasonality concerns. Population data for El Paso is for the county as the city population not available for 1890.

Table 2 – Regional Variation in Examinations

	Banks	Exam length (days)		Time since prior exam (days)		
		Mean	Median	Bottom quartile	Median	Top quartile
Overall	206	2.9	2	207	287	373
By size						
Larger banks	103	3.3	3	202	270	371
Smaller banks	103	2.6	2	208	314	376
By reserve city status						
Country bank	130	2.8	2	212	319	380
Reserve city bank	76	3.0	3	198	245	314
By region						
Ohio River Valley/South (OH, IA, KY, TN, LA, AL)	71	2.1	2	209	264	303
Plains (IA, MN, MO, NE, ND)	56	2.8	2	184	314	373
Mountain/Southwest (CO, MT, NM, TX, UT, WY)	50	3.8	4	197	316	382
Pacific (CA, OR, WA)	29	3.6	3	328	382	409

Table 3
Governance Indicators (means)

	Board size	Indep. directors as a share of Board	Share of loans to indep. directors	Share of banks w/ Active discount committee	Salary of President	Share of banks w/ Cashier bonded
Overall	9.1	69.5	5.4	59.7	$4,400	57
By size						
Larger banks	10.4	73.1	4.5	65.4	$5,900	56
Smaller banks	7.9	65.7	6.3	53.9	$2,500	59
By reserve city status						
Country bank	8.9	67.3	6.0	49.6	$3,300	52
Reserve city bank	9.6	73.2	4.6	78.9	$6,100	67
By region						
Ohio River Valley/South (OH, IA, KY, TN, LA, AL)	9.6	74.8	5.4	84.5	$4,800	70
Plains (IA, MN, MO, NE, ND)	10.0	70.3	4.6	62.5	$4,600	71
Mountain/Southwest (CO, MT, NM, TX, UT, WY)	8.6	65.0	6.5	30.0	$4,200	34
Pacific (CA, OR, WA)	7.2	62.6	5.0	44.8	$3,200	38

Table 4
Occupations of the Independent Shareholders

	Share of total
Capitalist	22.8
Merchant (wholesale)*	13.2
Merchant*	8.4
Lawyer	7.1
Mining or commodities	4.0
Banker (at other bank)	3.7
Real estate	3.5
Manufacturer	3.1
Other finance	2.1
Railroad	1.5
Farmer or rancher	1.3
Other	29.3

*These should be thought of as lower bounds on the share of individuals engaged in these professions. Many individuals are listed according to the particular product they sold.

Table 5

Independent Director Control and Borrowing

	Share of loans that were made to independent directors at banks with below average (median) control by independent directors (percent)	Share of loans that were made to independent directors at banks with above average (median) control by independent directors (percent)
Control measured by size of bank board of directors	4.5	7.7
Control measured by proportion of board consisting of independent directors	4.4	6.6
Control measure by stock ownership of independent directors	5.2	5.7

Table 6

Board of Directors Meeting Frequency

	Share of sample
Weekly	14
Twice monthly	10
Monthly	35
Quarterly	14
Semi-annual	8
Regular	4
Irregular	8
Other	7

Table 7
The Loan Book

	Demand loans to total loans	Share of banks w/ excessive loans	Troubled loans to all loans	Share of banks habitually allowing overdrafts	Share of banks with mortgage loans	Real estate loans to total loans
Overall	12.7	55	9.1	47	70	3.6
By size						
Larger banks	14.5	55	6.5	45	46	2.3
Smaller banks	10.5	56	11.8	47	46	4.9
By reserve city status						
Country bank	11.6	64	11.5	54	70	4.6
Reserve city bank	14.6	41	5.1	29	70	1.9
By region						
Ohio River Valley/South (OH, IA, KY, TN, LA, AL)	15.0	37	5.4	39	62	1.9
Plains (IA, MN, MO, NE, ND)	9.2	50	6.7	24	70	2.2
Mountain/Southwest (CO, MT, NM, TX, UT, WY)	8.2	78	14.1	84	80	5.4
Pacific (CA, OR, WA)	21.6	72	14.7	43	72	7.3

Table 8
Dividends and Writedowns

	Share of banks that paid dividends in past 6 months	Dividends per share	Share of banks that wrote off losses in past 6 months
Overall	69	$4.9	53
By size			
Larger banks	80	$4.0	66
Smaller banks	58	$6.0	41
By reserve city status			
Country bank	67	$5.5	51
Reserve city bank	72	$3.8	57
By region			
Ohio River Valley/South (OH, IA, KY, TN, LA, AL)	80	$4.1	63
Plains (IA, MN, MO, NE, ND)	70	$3.7	52
Mountain/Southwest (CO, MT, NM, TX, UT, WY)	66	$6.0	54
Pacific (CA, OR, WA)	45	$9.1	31

Table 9
Liabilities

	Ratio of checking to individual deposits	Ratio of time and demand certificates individual deposits	Rate on CDs to individuals	Share banks borrowing via CDs	Share banks borrowing from banks in any form
Overall	74	24	4.0	15	34
By size					
Larger banks	77	22	3.5	10	24
Smaller banks	72	27	4.4	20	44
By reserve city status					
Country bank	71	27	4.4	16	34
Reserve city bank	77	20	3.3	14	33
By region					
Ohio River Valley/South (OH, IA, KY, TN, LA, AL)	86	13	3.0	4	33
Plains (IA, MN, MO, NE, ND)	63	35	4.0	12	32
Mountain/Southwest (CO, MT, NM, TX, UT, WY)	73	25	4.5	21	28
Pacific (CA, OR, WA)	67	30	5.3	34	48

Table 10
Losses and recapitulation

	Ratio of losses to surplus and profits (median)	Ratio of loan losses to total losses (median)	Estimated loss rate on loans (median)	Share of exams where mgmt. criticized	Share of exams where assets criticized
Overall	4.0	90	10	9	17
By size					
Larger banks	2.4	100	18	5	10
Smaller banks	6.2	84	7	13	24
By reserve city status					
Country bank	4.6	85	10	9	19
Reserve city bank	2.7	94	13	8	12
By region					
Ohio River Valley/South (OH, IA, KY, TN, LA, AL)	2.0	100	10	4	8
Plains (IA, MN, MO, NE, ND)	4.2	87	18	9	18
Mountain/Southwest (CO, MT, NM, TX, UT, WY)	7.3	84	3	8	27
Pacific (CA, OR, WA)	5.7	81	14	21	17

Figure 1A – Distribution of ownership by management

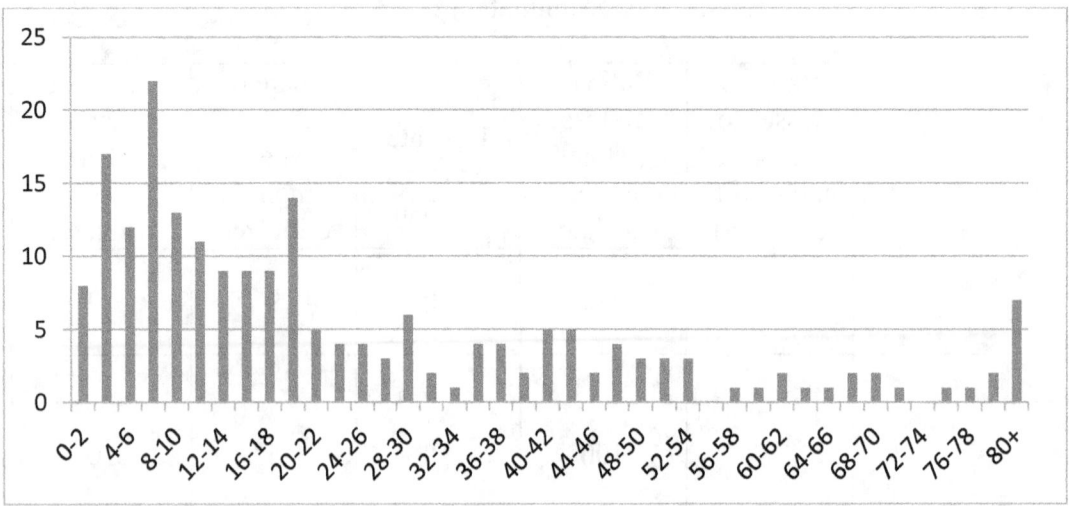

Figure 1B – Distribution of ownership by independent directors

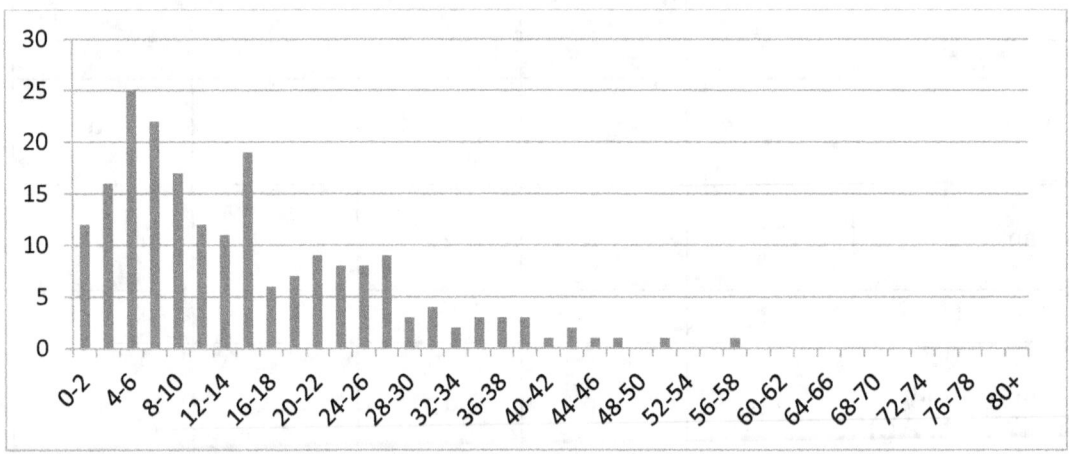

Figure 1C – Distribution of ownership by outsiders

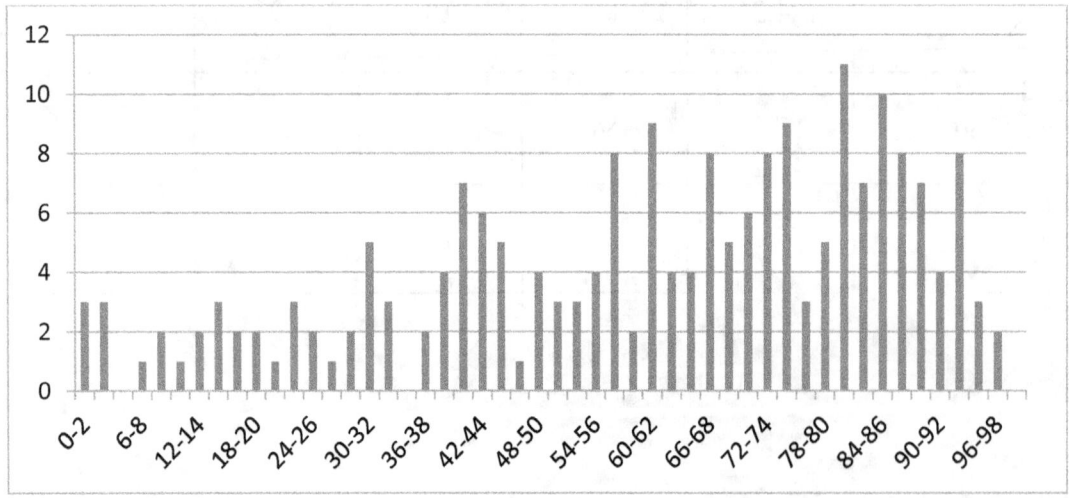

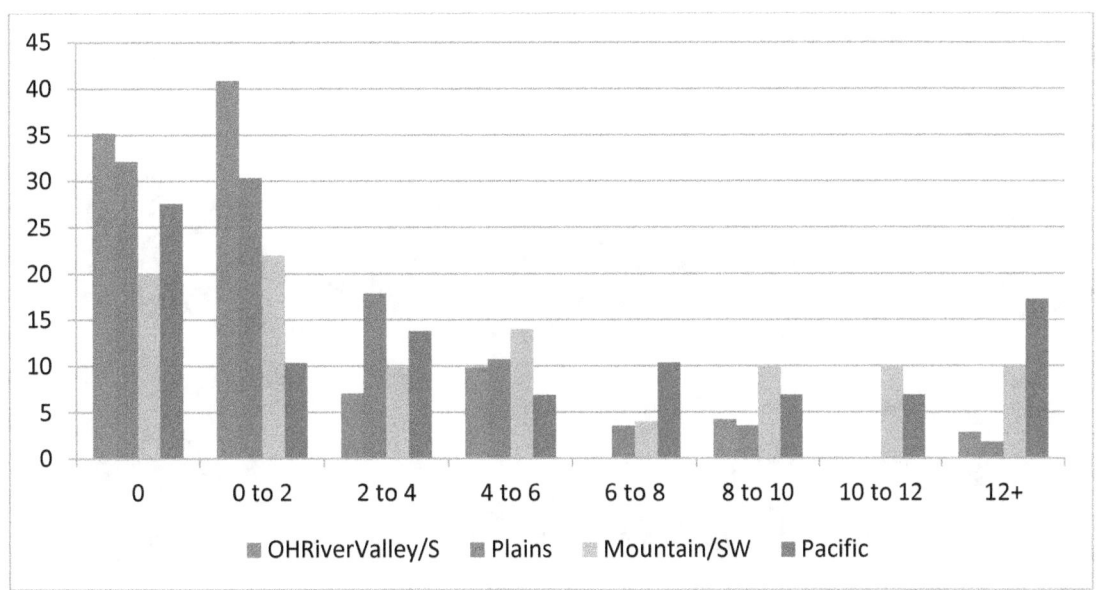

Figure 2
Distribution of real estate loans as a share of all loans

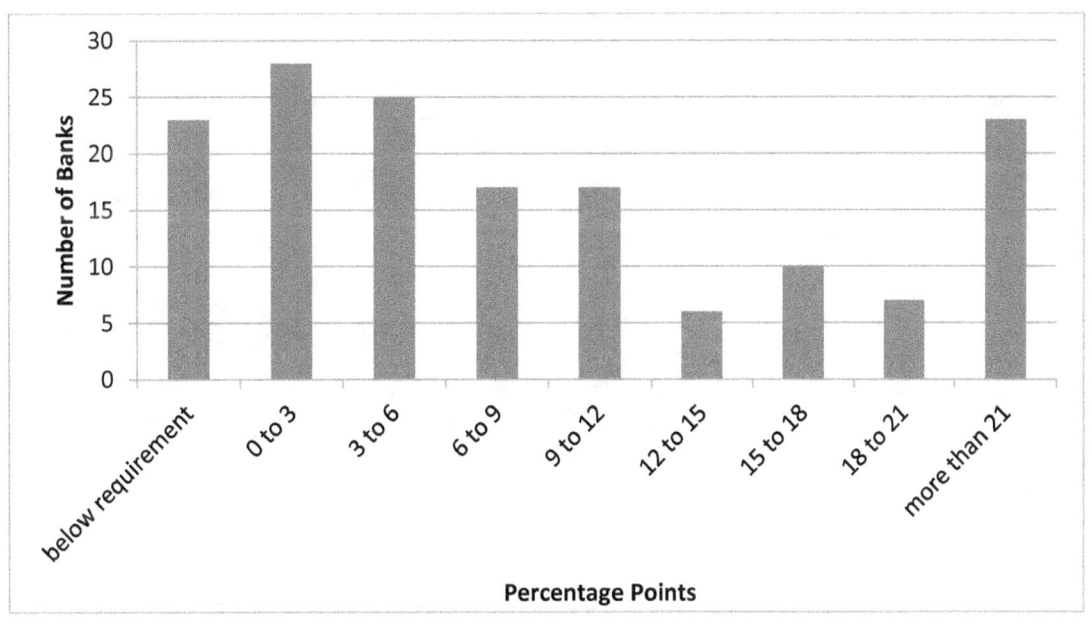

Figure 3
Distribution of reserves in excess of what was legally required

Figure 4
Share of banks using borrowed funds by month of exam report

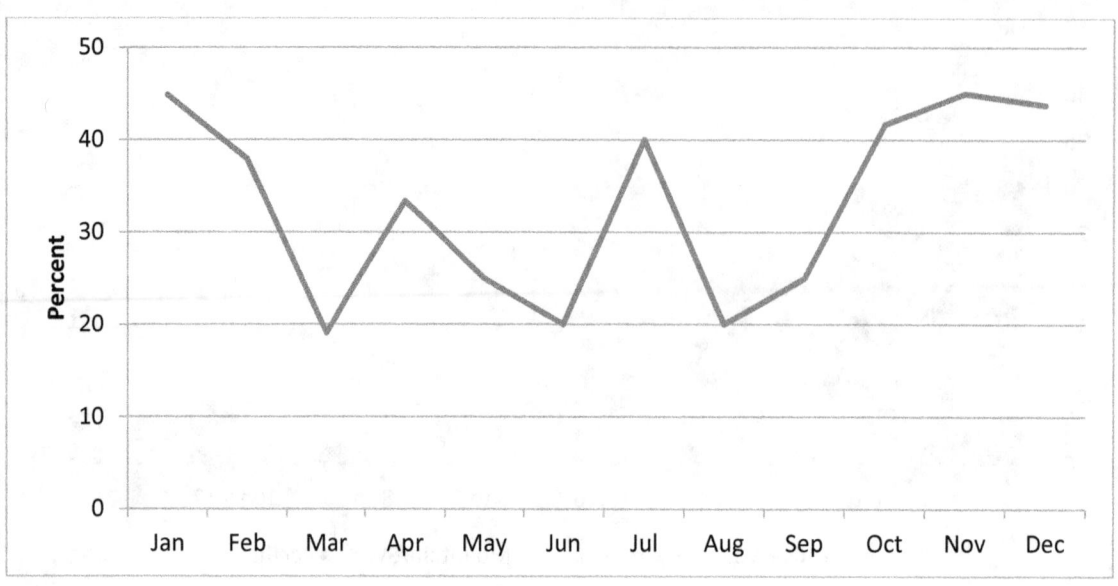